CW00507507

THEIR ABC:
INSIDE AUSTRALIA'S
LARGEST SHELTERED WORKSHOP

Their ABC: Inside Australia's Largest Sheltered Workshop

Published in 2022 by Connor Court Publishing Pty Ltd

Copyright © Richard Alston

All rights reserved. No part of this book may be reproduced or transmitted in any form or by any means, electronic or mechanical, including photo copying, recording or by any information storage and retrieval system, without prior permission in writing from the publisher.

Connor Court Publishing Pty Ltd
PO Box 7257
Redland Bay QLD 4165
sales@connorcourt.com
www.connorcourt.com
Phone 0497-900-685

Printed in Australia

ISBN: 9781922815071

Front cover design: Maria Giordano

THEIR ABC

INSIDE AUSTRALIA'S
LARGEST SHELTERED WORKSHOP

HON RICHARD ALSTON AO

Connor Court Publishing

"Taken to its logical conclusion, producer independence was an anarchist's charter... An ABC captured by the producers would serve the interests and reflect the prejudices of its staff rather than its listeners". -- NICK CATER

CONTENTS

INTRODUCTION

Growing up in the mid-20th century, I have fond memories of the ABC as a venerable institution. My parents started with nothing, including no tertiary education, yet they both had profound respect for the organisation and identified with its values.

The ABC exuded an air of authority and prided itself on being a journal of record. An obvious feature was senior management longevity, with Sir Charles Moses serving as General Manager from 1935 until 1965 and Sir Talbot Duckmanton from 1965 until 1982 – two general managers in almost fifty years. There was no doubt about who ran the place – senior management, and the board set the direction of travel.

It did not seek to compete with the commercial broadcasters, but rather to complement them, with quality programs. No doubt it upset the Government of the day from time to time but, in an honourable patriotic tradition, not as a policy crusader.

This was very much in line with the ideals of John Reith, the founding Director-General of the BBC, upon which the ABC was modelled. He considered that broadcasting had a responsibility to reflect and strengthen what he called "the spirit of common sense Christian ethics which we believe to be a necessary component of citizenship and culture".

His ideal of broadcasting to educate the masses framed the BBC and similar organisations around the world. Reith was conservative, but he quickly realised the importance of having trade union and Labour voices on the airwaves. His stance was seen as pivotal in establishing the BBC's reputation for impartiality.

As Henry Ergas has pointed out, Reith, in his 1924 manifesto, Broadcasting over Britain, said that the goal was not to impose high culture on the great unwashed; it was to provide "all men an atmosphere where they may use ideas", while being "nourished and not bound by them".

The ABC was started shortly after the BBC and followed in its footsteps but has since clearly lost its way. Having started life in the depths of the great depression one would expect that the ABC would be acutely aware of the misery and deprivation that was then the plight of ordinary Australians.

Nearly a century later, it is changed beyond recognition – rarely interested in the joys and struggles of the middle class, instead it revels in parading its elite, inner urban values – appealing to people like themselves.

The ABC's longest serving Chairman, Richard Boyer, was appointed by the Labor government in 1946 and shortly afterwards set out his stall: The national broadcaster should be "running no campaign, seeking to persuade no opinion, but presenting the issues freely and fearlessly for the calm judgment of our people ... (serving) as a much needed centre of national unity".

This mission statement is still valid today, or ought to be. As Charles Moore, writing in the UK's *The Telegraph* says: "The media – as the word implies – are supposed to be conveyors of accurate news to the public, rather than players in the drama. But in the Westminster village, that is considered boring. Particular contempt is felt, for example, for the basic duty of reporting what gets said in the Chamber of the House of Commons or the details of what a Bill contains".

Much more exciting to get hold of a Cabinet split, ministerial gaffe or example of "sleaze". This is what gets you promoted. This brings out the tendency – innate in most professions – to seek the esteem of colleagues rather than to serve the public. And, later: "Once again, the foetid air of Westminster intrigue, hypocrisy and moralism stifles the important things we need to know about our country and our world in these weird times".

Unfortunately the Westminster virus has been prevalent on our shores for many moons, getting worse not better. No wonder many now prefer the SBS news to its pallid, pretentious and parochial counterpart.

By the time Boyer died in 1961, however, a revolution was underway to rebrand the ABC and provoke more controversy. The emergence of the genre of television current affairs brought a new breed of young thrusters, endowed with unprecedented editorial freedom, determined to shake things up.

But, as Nick Cater has subsequently written: "Taken to its logical conclusion, producer independence was an anarchist's charter... An ABC captured by the producers would serve the interests and reflect the prejudices of its staff rather than its listeners".

This Day Tonight, launched in 1967,was fronted by Bill Peach, who later admitted that the show was "outrageously self-indulgent... (we) believed we knew everything". There seems to be ample evidence that this state of affairs is alive, if not well, today. The answer would seem to be an amendment to the ABC's statutory Charter to restore stakeholder accountability.

Unfortunately, with the passage of time, the national broadcaster has strayed far from Boyer's central tenet. It now makes no attempt to conceal its distaste for all things conservative and steadfastly refuses to employ any journalists with any such overt leanings. While imbued with self-righteous concepts of social justice morality, its leading journalists are almost uniformly well educated, middle-class and left-wing, having convinced themselves that politicians, especially of the Liberal variety, are little better than charlatans, ready to say or do anything to stay in power and utterly disinterested in the general welfare.

Today's ABC is unrecognisable from its first incarnation. It prefers to preach and cajole rather than inform and educate the masses. Management no longer call the shots. The current Managing Director, David Anderson, is nominally the editor-in-chief but, like his earlier predecessor, Mark Scott, he is either too busy or disinclined to rein in the wild horses; as a result, key journalists such as Sarah Ferguson, Louise Milligan and Caro Meldrum-Hanna would seem to be essentially left to their own devices, free to promote their own pet topics and political viewpoints.

They no longer regard themselves as reporters; many, such as Fran Kelly, are proud to be seen as political agitators, thereby turning what is supposed to be an impartial, fair and unbiased broadcaster into a recognisably political organisation.

The ABC prides itself on being a constant source of political controversy, in the process creating a fundamental dissonance with middle Australia, the heart of the nation – a far cry from its official mandate.

The Australian community essentially supports public broadcasting. But it also expects, as does the ABC Charter, that it should be impartial, efficient and audience-responsive. A very good starting place would be structural reform.

THE LAST GREAT PUBLIC SECTOR PROTECTION RACKET

The biggest problem is not only systemic bias, egregious as that is, but its flawed business model, which makes it a chronic underperformer on many fronts and increasingly irrelevant to the daily lives of its audience. Unlike its commercial counterparts, it is not exposed to competitive forces and therefore has no incentive to cater for its audience or trim the fat – it is simply not fighting fit.

Its workforce abides in a cosy, protected environment, where jobs are not at risk, (even during a pandemic), its income just keeps rolling in, leading journalists are virtually free to do as they like and it has no real competitors. But the price of absolute protection is a very high one, for both taxpayers and audiences.

Australia, and many of its post-war counterparts, once thought that all round protection was a great idea, as it shielded Australian businesses from foreign competition and the threat of going out of business. But, over time, the flaws, costs and inefficiencies of protection became manifest, both in Australia and the rest of the world.

The United States has now dominated the world stage for more than a century. Its success has been no accident, and other countries have sought to emulate its economic paradigm, with China adopting the highly successful model of modern capitalism, albeit "with Chinese characteristics". It can be brutal at times but Schumpeter's famous formula of "creative destruction", as the key to innovation and progress, is constantly in evidence.

Even mega corporations must prosper or perish – there is no standing still. And in order to do so they must be relentless innovators, with large Research and Development budgets. Chinese behemoth, Huawei, boasts that almost half of its 80,000 workforce is employed in R & D.

The Chinese, as do their American counterparts, know that constant re-invention is the key to success and have poured vast resources into new technologies in order to stay ahead of the competition.

Without the motivating force of competition all businesses get lazy. The same goes for public sector businesses. The Labor party recognised this in the Hawke-Keating era when they privatised almost everything that moved, leaving it to the Howard Government to do the same with Telstra.

The case against corporate protectionism is now beyond dispute but its vices apply equally to the public sector. It allows inefficiency and overstaffing to flourish and provides no incentives for technical and business improvement, let alone innovation and striving for excellence.

A protected ABC can also afford to become sloppy – it used to have a pronunciation committee, but clearly no longer. Time and again Melbourne audiences have to listen to mispronunciations of Victorian towns.

Instead of making high quality home-made histories and drama it prefers the lazy option of endless BBC re-treads – good as many are – and pursuing ever more digital upgrades and mindless comedy and games shows, in the mistaken belief that it must cater principally for the younger demographic – supposedly the audience of tomorrow. But, as the BBC is rapidly learning with a similar strategy, in doing so it is risking not just its core audience but its very identity. It is not as if the youth market is being ignored by the commercial sector so, again, the ABC is competing with, not complementing, the commercials.

Perhaps the greatest proof of the dysfunctionality of the ABC model, as a result of living behind its gilded protectionist barrier, is that it is able to get away with deliberately alienating at least half of its addressable audience – those who don't share its "progressive" left of centre worldview – who are nevertheless, as taxpayers, required to subsidise this grotesque lack of return on their investment. No commercial organisation, having to compete in the real world, would even think of doing such a thing.

At a time when commercial media companies are fighting for their lives to withstand the tidal wave of digitisation and the deadly predations of gargantuan high tech platforms and having to impose never ending labour force cutbacks, the ABC sails serenely on, content to simply plead for ever more corporate welfare.

Who will ever forget the outrageous toadying of the then newly installed Managing Director, David Anderson, ahead of the 2019 Federal election, going public to effectively advocate a vote against the Coalition Government for its lack of financial generosity. No doubt it helped to establish his hero status amongst the troops, but this is certainly not what the Managing Director is paid to do.

Being Australia's largest sheltered workshop means not only never having to say you're sorry, but never having to earn a living – classic sit-down money. It is now the biggest media outlet in Australia, with guaranteed income in excess of $1 billion and under no threat from any competitors – the largest moat in the world.

Meanwhile the commercial media sector has to cater for its

readers and audience or go out of business. It is tested daily in the market place, unlike the ABC, which is not dependent on ratings for advertising revenue – just a guaranteed billion dollar annual handout, for which it is largely unaccountable, and certainly not to its consumers.

Economic concepts such as productive efficiency and performance review are now well accepted by both the Liberal and Labor parties. About 12 months ago David Anderson realised that paying bonuses during the pandemic was not a good look but it was only a tactical withdrawal as bonus payments have since been resumed – to the tune of more than $300,000, including $144,000 to a senior executive. But taxpayers are none the wiser about the need or merit for such largesse-essentially for doing their day job.

Unlike public companies, which have to account to shareholders at AGM time, the ABC refuses to publish audience numbers for particular programs, especially the news and current affairs component. These statistics are vital to ensuring that the ABC audience is meeting the needs of its audience and justifying the extraordinary largesse bestowed annually on it. The ABC likes to pretend that these figures are "commercial in confidence" although it is not involved in any commercial activities

Once privatised, Telstra's workforce halved, demonstrating that market scrutiny and competitor pressure deliver efficiencies. In many respects the ABC is Australia's last "natural monopoly".

One of the most useful measures for investors is to look for companies where senior management have a significant shareholding in the enterprise – skin in the game. They then have a vested interest in financial success and if they don't perform they can be dismissed. But most ABC employees don't know how to define success, other than in personal terms. In fact, no one could formulate a success formula, apart from getting "more money than last time".

In the public service the culture is quite different – loyalty means shared, often political, values. The ABC doesn't have to worry about pesky shareholders, difficult AGMs or M & A predators. None of its senior executives or journalists have any financial or other incentive for seeing their employer prosper, so they are free to get their kicks by being sole traders, pursuing personal ambitions and chasing their own policy windmills.

The ABC budget allocation is like a glorified defined benefit scheme where you get your reward irrespective of employee performance or employer capacity to pay. Such schemes belong to a bygone era, yet the ABC shows no awareness of its very special status or its great good fortune in being insulated from the existential forces besetting the commercial media sector.

The ABC funding package from the Parliament is always higher than last time – not taking account of belt tightening elsewhere, or its own achievements – no nasty KPIs to meet. Yet the ABC simply refuses to disclose audience figures or any other relevant indicators of "success".

At the same time it is quite uninterested in trying to raise money from the private or philanthropic sectors, no doubt for fear it might jeopardise its annual parliamentary handouts. It could, of course, strike a deal to legislatively ring fence its annual handout, but the staff politics would probably be deadly in an inmates-run organisation.

Another feature of a protected monopoly is that it is not under any pressure to keep its labour force numbers as low as possible. It took years for it to stop sending reporters from multiple ABC units to attend the same press conference.

ABC staffing levels, now close to 4000, remain almost static. At the height of the pandemic in mid-2020 the ABC announced that 250 jobs would go but did not mention that it would be spread over three years and would most likely be achieved by voluntary redundancies.

No one ever seems to get sacked and if some are quietly made redundant there is no pressure to be other than very generous, perhaps accompanied by a non-disclosure agreement so the taxpayer is none the wiser.

A classic example of over staffing is the number of in-house lawyers, which has doubled over the last decade to 28 and counting, as it has recently been advertising for more. Other media organisations would typically have less than ten. It is not surprising that one leading media executive has described the ABC lawyer complement as "woefully bloated".

It doesn't stop there. The ABC is also free to spend large amounts on the best, and most expensive, barristers and solicitors in the commercial marketplace.

In the Christian Porter case, the ABC reportedly made an initial provision of $700,000 and was prepared to spend another $2 million. It had already retained the services of one of the best and most expensive QCs (and an experienced junior) in the business. This is not just about defence, more about intimidation – "pour encourager les autres".

We are all very familiar with the prolonged death throes – shrinking newspaper size, reduced pages and content quality – which beset the Fairfax group until it was absorbed by the Nine Network. The gilded monopoly that is the ABC has never had to face any of these existential challenges. Nor has it ever had to worry about being put out of business by tech platform giants or social media.

Another insidious feature of being a protected species is the role of the staff-appointed board director, a position unheard of in the real world. This position of in-house "mole" constitutes a fundamental conflict of interest, as staff expect their interests to be prioritised and to be briefed about board matters which could be quite sensitive. Anything of serious concern can be quickly leaked to sympathetic media. All this has a stifling effect on open and free flowing boardroom discussion, and ultimately the performance of the enterprise.

Companies without competition decline in quality. They are under no pressure to innovate or look for cost saving initiatives and best practice strategies. They can simply concentrate on empire-building and self-aggrandisement.

Another vice of all-round protection is that the protected entity becomes impervious to criticism – thus the ABC feels under no obligation to seriously interact with its viewers and listeners or honour its accountability obligations to the Parliament.

Over many years there has been much, mostly well-directed, criticism of the ABC in relation to its political journalism. The striking feature of its response to any criticism has been its complete disdain for its critics, be they from government, Parliament, the regulators or the general public. This is a dysfunctional outcome; every other organisation, and its employees, is beholden to its stakeholders.

Its usual strategy is to say nothing, lie low and then carry on as if nothing has happened. Accordingly, it never learns from its mistakes and as a result forfeits the trust of many of its long suffering viewers and listeners, as evidenced by the precipitous decline in audience numbers.

It is easy to blame the uniform left-of-centre worldview – more green or humanistic than overtly party political – but I believe the answer is fundamentally structural. The business model is fatally flawed.

One of the ABC's favourite sons, Professor Julius Sumner Miller, used to ask: "Why is it so?" In this case, the answer seems to be that its senior journalists are overwhelmingly middle class and tertiary educated, often products of left wing media studies courses, inner city residents with little or no commercial or even private sector experience. They are infected by group think and loyalty to each other, with little concern for the organisation's success or reputation.

Over the years they have diverged ever further from classical liberalism, which until a generation or so ago was conventional wisdom, although even then its adherents were probably confined to a select few inside the ABC.

Two political philosophers attached to the American Enterprise Institute, Benjamin and Jenna Silber Storey, offer this explanation of societal drift: "The political institutions of liberalism were designed for people who were strongly committed to churches, localities, professions and families. But when private lives have broken down – families dissolved, localities less important, religious life absent – liberalism's framework and institutions no longer make sense". Thus the ABC has seen a continuing drift from Christian, middle class values towards the humanist and the secular.

What Ita Buttrose and co don't seem to realise is that the ABC's elitist values and its monolithic world view are not respected, let alone shared, by the majority of Australians. If she does, then keeping quiet about it certainly won't change the organisational ethos.

It likes to pretend that internal polling, which it always refuses to publicly release, shows that Australians support the ABC – in the broad. It claims to do well in regional and rural Australia, where local staff live and reflect local values, but a recent survey conducted by Compass Polling for the Page Research Institute suggests the ABC is almost irrelevant to most daily lives outside the cities, offering little of value that can't be found elsewhere. Only 20% tune into ABC local radio at least once per week and only 8% listen to Radio National. Instead they tune into commercial radio (35%), podcasts (12%) and internet radio (10%).

The ABC likes to claim that it is Australia's most trusted news source, yet, on the main evening TV news bulletins, it regularly comes third behind Channels 7 and 9. The ABC has never contested published reports that the audience for the ABC news and *The 7.30* has halved in Sydney and Melbourne over the past ten years, while the population has increased by more than 20 per cent. Over that period even its once prestigious *Lateline* program outstayed its welcome.

When it emerged in May 2018 that viewer numbers had fallen by 100,0000, or 12 per cent in the previous twelve months, the ABC's lame answer was that their journalists needed more training. This was real head in the sand stuff, as it would have known from privately commissioned research that increasing swathes of previously rusted-on viewers had simply had enough of continued, and increasingly irrelevant, mediocrity.

7.30, once the current affairs flagship, is not as penetrating as it once was. While the ABC idea of news is little more than an embarrassment – very parochial, it doesn't even have a proper national news, just a series of largely state focussed stories.

Paul Keating well remembers the ABC's glory days and regrets the dumbing down of its news and current affairs offerings. As he has pointed out: "too many tragic reports, of no broader consequence".

What you get on the ABC is "A truck has just overturned on the Pacific Highway". The commercials serve this stuff up all the time – what is the ABC's point of difference?

I suspect the reason for this apparent laziness is that police rounds make this vacuous stuff available free of charge, as do the unions, who provide the ABC with endless worker's hard luck stories. We never get thoughtful analysis from the *7.30* – few hard questions (except to conservative politicians), let alone serious policy alternatives.

Meanwhile, SBS, with a much smaller budget, manages to produce a quality one hour news program each night, with international stories often leading the way.

COVID has proved a content godsend to the ABC, allowing to deliver virtually nothing else – every night, just wall to wall case numbers and accompanying "hard luck" stories, which do not tell anything like the whole story, but always fearful rather than positive. Again this material is tendentiously served up on a platter from the usual suspects, replete with Daniel Andrews' preferred slant. We all have sympathy for obvious victims, but that is no excuse for one of the nation's leading broadcasters to wallow in a diet of endless "compassion".

WHY THIS PERSISTENT POLITICAL MYOPIA?

The fundamental problem, verging on the existential, is that the ABC current affairs (aka politics) units are at war with many of its viewers.

The ABC simply refuses to concede mistakes, thumbs its nose at any adverse finding by regulators or outside reviewers, doubles down at every opportunity and boasts that its "independence" means it can do what it likes, irrespective of its charter obligation to be fair and impartial.

Its latest act of defiance is an essay by its Managing Director David Anderson screaming "the critics don't deter us". His "take-no-prisoners" philippic is no doubt designed to reassure the insiders, whose hard core, anti-Coalition world view prevails unchallenged and helps to keep his position safe. He makes no attempt to deal with any substantial form of criticism and his "rant" has predictably sunk without trace, even in the wider media.

Not much better is another dreadfully one sided effort entitled *Who Needs the ABC?* It is not clear who commissioned this piece of sludge, but it came out coincidentally ahead of the Federal election and mirrors all of the ABC's main complaints.

One of its main grievances is the never ending winge about funding cuts. The essence of this argument is that the ABC is sacrosanct and should never lose a single dollar, irrespective of performance, competing demands such as the need for a massive increase in the Defence budget or dramatic changes in the media landscape which are threatening all other media players. The authors claim that job losses have been driven by deliberate and repeated budget cuts orchestrated by government. In other words the ABC is entitled to never have to cut jobs even though the digital revolution has rendered many positions obsolete. As Nick Cater has pointed out, despite embarking on a digital makeover almost 15 years ago, the ABC's iview audience trails a long way behind its competitors despite offering its services for free.

The authors are not shy of hyperbole – the Government wants the ABC not to utter the words "climate change" and "policy" in the same sentence or ask about women in Liberal-National Party ranks. These claims are so risible that they hardly need refutation.

They also have the temerity to claim, without any supporting evidence, that both sides of politics "loathe the ABC" and would like to see it privatised – a favourite Aunt Sally. This is dead wrong – both sides want a high-quality, fair and impartial national broadcaster which adheres to its Charter. It is ironic that many erstwhile rusted-on ABC viewers have abandoned its news offerings in disgust, preferring the SBS offering.

The mere fact that the ABC comes under intense criticism at times is supposed to be proof positive that all this is wrong and unfair – "what we are concerned about is the attack on a valuable cultural institution." This is shades of "my country right or wrong" and not far removed from a call for cancel culture – no attempt to analyse whether any criticism is justified, let alone do something about it. The ultimate in denial is this pearler: "It is not necessarily a problem that the ABC's reporting attracts heat – that's an inevitable result of good journalism".

These hysterical outpourings do the ABC no good – they simply demonstrate that some of its supporters are immune to reason and rationality.

More than twenty five years ago Christopher Lasch, an American cultural historian and disillusioned man of the Left, wrote a best seller, *The Revolt of the Elites and the Betrayal of Democracy*, in which he excoriated the breed. Living in enclaves and comfortably isolated inside their own networks, they had abandoned the middle class, divided the nation, scorned religion and betrayed the very idea of democracy. The radical left agenda had become mostly a blind for moralistic self-indulgence.

This description fits the ABC to a tee. The great majority of its staff work in the comfortable inner city enclaves of Ultimo in Sydney and Southbank in Melbourne. It would be very surprising if they watch Sky News or read Peta Credlin or know anyone who does. They much prefer to live in Greensland. It is not necessarily a deliberately ALP view but there is little doubt which of the major parties they prefer.

 It is more of a green tinged, faux-social justice view, largely devoid of any understanding of the workings of government, let alone the complexities involved. This innate moral superiority complex not only leads its most prominent journalists to be constantly critical of almost everything that Federal governments, especially Coalition ones, do or say, but it also happens to provide an inexhaustible supply of cheap political ammunition to fill up the airwaves.

Elites are typically comfortable, detached citizens of the world and leading ABC journalists display all the obsessions of those who are mostly insulated from the realities of ordinary lives – unlike politicians, especially those representing marginal electorates, who are acutely aware of the travails of their constituents and the real world they live in.

Untroubled by these concerns, most prominent ABC journalists show little interest in economic issues, remaining fixated on progressive social issues such as gender diversity, discrimination, climate change, gay marriage and asylum seekers, as well as an unrelieved diet of anti-Trumpism. They judge the rest of the community by their own standards and values and therefore have no idea of, or interest in, how the other half lives.

The rise of Donald Trump graphically demonstrated that middle America had no interest in Hillary Clinton's hot button issues and the same is undoubtedly the case in middle Australia. Yet the ABC, and especially "star" journalists, remain bewildered at how so many Americans got it so wrong for so long – and still do.

This is not the first time the ABC's disdain for the middle class has led it astray. It constantly shrieked at every word from Pauline Hanson, without ever pausing to reflect on the real reasons for her support, which it lazily and reflexively put down to racism.

About 25 years ago, when I first became the Minister responsible for the ABC, the place was an economics-free zone, happy to provide wall to wall coverage of politics, but economics was a no-go area – they simply weren't interested.

Little has changed since then. It is simply incomprehensible that, in the depths of the Covid crisis, Emma Alberici, its "principal economics correspondent", could urge people to "stop talking about the economy", as though it was some abstract concept, rather than the lifeblood of the nation. Fortunately, she was moved on shortly afterwards, but the damage to the ABC was there for all the world to see.

The reality is that, presumably apart from its finance department, no one in the ABC is much interested in economics or economic principles such as cost-benefit analysis – their overriding interest is in playing the political game, but from the safety of the sidelines.

Barry Cassidy and Kerry O'Brien might have gained some first-hand experience in politics from working with Bob Hawke and Gough Whitlam respectively, but it only re-enforced their adamantine left-wing world view. Otherwise most ABC commentators and journalists are simply roadside observers.

They have little or no interest in understanding the need for political compromise or how the democratic process works, let alone exploring who should bear the burden of higher taxes, which is the inevitable implication of their constant demands for government to do ever more. They would much prefer to spend their time "holding government to account", which is simply code for being constant critics. The responsibility of reporters is to inform an audience of what is happening, hopefully accompanied by some cogent analysis; accountability is the responsibility of the Parliament.

Q &A is the standout offender when it comes to one sided presentations. Nothing much has changed since Tom Switzer pointed out a few years ago: "On topics such as refugees, gay marriage and climate change its coverage is loaded. Its choice of guests is always unbalanced. Its former host Tony Jones was incorrigibly biased. It employs double standards in treating conservatives far more roughly than the other guests. Much of its questioning rests on a series of leftist ideological assumptions. All of this, moreover, is in front of a studio audience which treats anyone who strays from the progressive consensus with shock and distaste".

Switzer has also provided a classic example of the prevailing double standards: "According to Tony Jones, the right wing Mark Steyn is a 'conservative polemicist', whereas the far left journalist Robert Fisk is 'one of the most experienced observers of the Middle East'. Enough said.

If the ABC has a political strategy it is this: never admit to bias; ignore almost every criticism that can be ignored; and constantly ask for more money.

People complain about the ferocity of Canberra politics where the stakes are sky high. But, in reality, the ABC is also intensely political – everything is contestable, every journalist seems to have a strong, if quaintly uniform, view. Kissinger's amusing aphorism that "university politics is so vicious because the stakes are so small" is only half-right when it comes to the ABC. The personal stakes for individual journalists might be small but the stakes for millions of Australian voters are anything but.

THE UNTOUCHABLES

As Gerard Henderson constantly points out, the ABC is a staff-run collective with silos such as *Four Corners* and *Q & A* virtually untouchable, as mistakes, during the reign of leading executive producer Sally Neighbour, have famously demonstrated. Because of the siege mentality and misguided sense of loyalty no one is game to challenge these petty tyrants. As a consequence no one is in charge.

For many years the Managing Director has been officially the Editor-in-Chief. But when it came to the voyeuristic and utterly politically irrelevant *Four Corners* hatchet job on two Cabinet ministers, the official Editor-in-Chief, David Anderson, simply abdicated all responsibility and made sure that Ita Buttrose wore the blame.

The ABC receives constant criticism for its left wing bias, yet it never, ever responds on the merits. It is happy to trot out disingenuous bromides like "everybody loves the ABC" or "if both sides of politics criticise us we must be doing something right". It simply ignores its critics, whether they come from official sources, such as ACMA, the independent regulator, or even from its own self-appointed bias reviewer.

Australia may be politically diverse – nearly every election outcome is close – but the same cannot be said for the ABC. One of its current obsessions is diversity, by which it means on all fronts except the political, where its views are overwhelmingly one-sided and always to the left. It is hard to keep a straight face when Fran Kelly point blank denies that the ABC has any left wing bias and Leigh Sales pretends that there may well be some conservatives at the ABC – presumably keeping their heads well down. Meanwhile, Barry Cassidy warns that to have any would be "dangerous"! The reality is that they have never wanted any other than token conservatives and, even then, usually of the soft left variety. To her credit, Leigh Sales has given both Daniel Andrews and Anthony Albanese a hard time and for her troubles has copped intense criticism from lefties on twitter. Lesson: Disengage from the twitterverse.

Despite Daniel Andrews' quarantine fiasco, leading to the loss of some 600 lives, his hiding behind a very unsatisfactory "judicial inquiry" and his unbelievable refusal to accept any responsibility, the ABC simply refused to lay a glove on him.

It accepted the Andrews Government line that the fact that Victoria had suffered around 90 per cent of all COVID deaths in Australia was just bad luck, rather than a poor contact tracing system. The ABC is an ardent lockdown advocate, although not adversely affected by it, so it is firmly on Andrews' side in preferencing health issues ahead of economic ones. Andrews' invariable media conference tactic is didactic, hide behind 'the science' and never engage in an explanation for hordes of petty restrictions, just offensive and unimaginative evasions like "we had no choice".

Yet the ABC is oblivious to these basic shortcomings, uninterested in exploring Andrews' appalling disregard and lack of concern for the economic devastation that his draconian lockdowns have had on jobs and small business, the engine of an economy's growth.

Perhaps this is understandable, if not acceptable. Those in secure public sector employment can hardly be expected to empathise with the vicissitudes of life faced by ordinary working class families. Much easier to try and scare the living daylights out of them with high but meaningless case numbers, ignoring remarkably low death numbers – nearly all aged in their 80s with multiple morbidities. Understandably, the punters see through all this and hence are willing to resort to occasional outbreaks of social disobedience.

THE ABC'S MUCH VAUNTED "INDEPENDENCE"

"Independence" is a favourite ABC catch cry – trotted out whenever it needs to deflect any serious criticism, perhaps drawing inspiration from Humpty Dumpty's witty apothegm: "When I use a word it means just what I choose it to mean – neither more or less".

This allows its left-media mates, including its "Friends of the ABC" acolytes and the relevant unions, to lazily follow suit, without bothering to examine the merits of the argument. Fortunately for the ABC, this hallowed term is mentioned several times, in the ABC Act, but never defined.

Unlike any private sector company, where such behaviour would not be tolerated, the ABC just rolls over when in-house staff such as its *Four Corners* clique Louise Milligan and Sally Neighbour have no compunction in biting the hand that feeds them. Similarly, a Trappist silence descends when one of their own such as Quentin Dempster attacks the Coalition Government, as he was frequently wont to do.

The Act makes it clear that the ABC is accountable to the Parliament and has strict obligations in terms of financial management reporting. There is no entitlement to any specific level of public funding and no formula for determining when enough's enough.

But there is a heavy duty imposed on the Government not to interfere in the day-to-day running of the Corporation and no government would dare to do so. This does not preclude criticism – daily fare for the ABC to dish out, but notoriously thin-skinned when it is on the receiving end.

SOCIAL MEDIA

In the wake of the recent Four Corners outbursts and the public criticism of her employer by Meldrum-Hanna over the Luna Park/ Wran "documentary", the ABC belatedly followed the BBC in moving to limit the use and abuse of social media by some of its leading "talent". Managing Director David Anderson has written to staff reminding them of recent high profile defamation cases which have been very costly for their employer.

Meanwhile, the real culprits managed to get off virtually scot-free (private counselling is a classic slap with a feather), despite Anderson bemoaning that such personal social media activity reflects badly on the ABC's independence and integrity.

But instead of simply banning personal postings, which by definition cannot be regarded as promoting the ABC cause, he limply said that staff should make it clear that "posts or likes are your personal view and do not represent the views of the ABC". This completely ignores the obvious fact that without their ABC association such self-indulgent staff musings would be of no interest to anyone. No other public or private sector employer would allow such licence.

Perhaps the ABC should take note of what is happening with the mothership. The BBC's new Director General, Tim Davie, is in the process of cracking down on staff virtue-signalling and bias by self-indulgent employees in an effort to "ensure the highest possible standards of impartiality".

The most obvious recent managerial dereliction was the unexplained decision by the Managing Director, acting alone without consulting the Board, that the ABC would not only pay damages of $79,000, but would indemnify Louise Milligan for her non-employment related outbursts. It could ultimately face substantial legal and Fringe Benefit Tax bills of close to $400,000 for her clearly unauthorised personal denigration of Andrew Laming MP. The Commonwealth Auditor-General later found that the ABC had "no policy or precedent" to support this decision.

This would not have happened in any other public body. In the private sector, directors are only indemnified for liability arising out of the conduct of the business or in the discharge of their directors' duties.

This episode is particularly egregious as the case could have been settled at the outset by the offer of an apology. Not only did Milligan and the ABC decline to do so but, instead, the ABC spared no expense in its haste to engage a leading international law firm and brief one of Melbourne's top defamation silks.

Unbelievably, it also gave Milligan a financial guarantee and had its communications department, led by her partner, Nick Leys, issue supportive statements on her behalf. No commercial firm would dream of acting in such a cavalier manner but the ABC, safe behind its impregnable $1 billion plus funding wall, does so because it can, knowing that there will be no stakeholder retribution.

When Milligan went down in a screaming heap, she neither apologised nor sought to explain her actions. As Chris Merritt explained in a timely article in *The Australian*, the national broadcaster is obliged to conduct itself as a model litigant. This obviously includes publicly accepting the umpire's verdict and apologising when it has conceded wrong-doing by agreeing to pay damages and costs to the plaintiff.

The likely explanation for this extraordinary and undeserved largesse, instead of a humble apology, is that the ABC was not prepared to risk Milligan's resignation. The public may well ask: "Is that what taxpayer funds are for?"

Another feature of the ABC's belated response to media storms of criticism is that it is very selective. Laura Tingle has never been reprimanded over her late night tweet accusing Scott Morrison of "ideological bastardry". And who will ever forget the ABC Board's deafening silence when Anderson went so outrageously off piste before the 2019 election.

But Anderson's position as Editor-in-Chief is an invidious one. Presumably for the same reasons, his predecessor but one, Mark Scott, declined to stand aside or appoint a replacement – the staff wouldn't cop an outsider being brought in. They much prefer a toothless insider, busy with myriad other matters, who ultimately lacks any real power to discipline, let alone dismiss.

These untouchables don't really want to run anything – how dull and time-consuming. They much prefer a cultural take-over, with the place being run on their terms and in accordance with their world view.

Given that the ABC, like a few other media outlets, was hopelessly wrong in its confident expectation of a Shorten election victory in 2019, the ABC's own commissioned Election Impartiality review, undertaken by former senior BBC journalist, Kerry Blackburn, makes interesting reading. The report was finally released by the ABC some 18 months after the election in question. Even then, it only did so after a Senate vote forced it to do so.

The report principally focused on two editions of *Insiders*, whose host, Barry Cassidy, had confidently predicted a Shorten victory, just as he had done with Mark Latham in 2004. It found that the 14 April 2019 episode was twice as likely to contribute to a favourable impression of Labor than the Coalition and by 12 May 2019 this over-confidence had blown out to 3.5 times.

It also found that "there was lively panel discussion about the Liberal Party launch…which was overwhelmingly negative for the Coalition" with "some poking of fun at the Liberal Prime Minister", but little at Labor.

Blackburn also found that *Insiders* should have secured more conservative-leaning political commentators as panellists, whose views would have articulated with conviction that there was a Coalition path to victory.

The Blackburn report also expressed concerns about the lack of plurality of political perspectives and named the nightly "news" program, *The Drum,* as the principal offender: in three of the five editions watched, there was a predominance of views which favoured Labor.

One episode of *The Drum* was labelled "one-sided", characterised by "not just a positive impression for policies identified with Labor's platform but also marked enthusiasm for a Labor victory".

What was the ABC's response? A furious objection, not only to the release on "public interest grounds" (as if the there was no public interest in the findings) but a point blank refusal to justify its blatant one sidedness at the most important time in the electoral cycle, let alone any suggestion of whether it proposed to do anything about the devastating findings of its own report. Needless to say, no corrective action was ever contemplated – just the usual hiding under the doona until the storm had passed.

This was a clear dereliction of duty by the board and senior management, no doubt fearful that it would provoke an internal revolt. Predictably, Barrie Cassidy, ever the warhorse, even in retirement, fulminated that the national broadcaster would be heading down "a dangerous path" if it were to actively recruit more conservative panellists. No explanation for his political prejudice, just self-evidently right. Such arrogant smugness simply confirms who really runs the ABC.

The organisation's continued intransigence was compounded by the release of a statement by Nick Leys, ABC Head of Communications. This utterly self-serving document made no attempt to address Blackburn's damning criticisms. Instead, it chose to cherry pick a few favourable comments, implying the report was a glowing endorsement of ABC editorial practices. Such evasive and disingenuous behaviour, presumably condoned at the highest levels, simply demonstrates why the ABC can no longer be trusted by the Australian public.

In the wake of the settlement of the Christian Porter defamation action the ABC admitted that it "did not contend that the serious accusations could be substantiated to the applicable legal standard – criminal or civil". Yet it was happy to engage top silks and run up large legal bills, because it could – with effectively no commercial constraints.

This has been labelled its 'money power shield' by Robert Gottliebsen, one of Australia's top commercial journalists, whereby its wealth pool becomes a weapon to intimidate actual and potential plaintiffs – hardly model litigant behaviour.

It is also extraordinary that the ABC claims to have no record of how much it has spent settling legal claims brought against it over the last six years. If true it is an astonishing admission of mismanagement. It could clearly find out by asking its lawyers, both in-house and external, but it is obviously fearful of the bad publicity which would attach to such public disclosure.

One of the ABC's primary Charter responsibilities is to inform its viewers and listeners. Yet in the Christian Porter fiasco it was happy to simply blacken the reputation of a very senior Cabinet minister on the basis of unproveable hearsay. It also proudly led the resulting media pile-on.

As Porter subsequently pointed out in his resignation press release: "The most frightening indicator that the public broadcaster was central in this shift to a presumption of guilt by media is the fact that the ABC – seemingly with great care and effort – has reported only those parts of the information in its possession which feeds the narrative of guilt". So much for its Code obligation to provide information that will enable the audience to make up their own minds.

 As if to demonstrate that they disapproved of the ABC capitulation in agreeing to settle the Porter case, both Milligan and Neighbour immediately and defiantly tweeted that they stood by their stories. They were clearly not interested in the welfare of the organisation or senior management's attempts to be both realistic and reasonable – they just preferred endless tribal warfare and self-justification, whatever the cost.

Not content with the hatchet job on Porter, the ABC followed up with another on former Labor Treasurer, John Dawkins, who was besmirched on very flimsy material, despite his strenuous denials and not being given any right to protest. Yet again, no apology.

Following an earlier episode, the Communications Minister, Paul Fletcher, wrote to the ABC chair accusing the Board of failing in its duty to ensure the broadcast of "accurate and impartial news and information".

Predictably, the ABC response was a lame attempt to change the subject, with Buttrose disingenuously complaining that she had been "disrespected", as if she had some regal entitlement to be beyond reproach. What about the disrespect the ABC habitually shows to its own viewers and listeners?

The other extraordinary freelance "documentary" operation at *Four Corners* was the despicable attempt to damn Neville Wran without any solid evidence, presumably because he was dead and couldn't sue. The Managing Director's risible defence was that the ABC was entitled to make unsubstantiated allegations.

Despite an independent enquiry, one of whose members was an ABC stalwart, Chris Masters, finding that the program was completely out of order and misled viewers, this judgment was treated with disdain by one of the key offenders, Caro Meldrum-Hanna, who "researched" the program.

Although the report had been commissioned by the ABC, its long serving Director, News, Analysis and Investigations, Gaven Morris, had the temerity to put out a press release saying the ABC rejected the findings and again trotted out the same lame excuse that they were entitled to publish unsupported allegations. Now that he has had enough and has left the organisation it will be interesting to discover in due course if there was any felt coercion on his part.

These repeated acts of defiance are simply outrageous – the ABC is determined never to learn from its mistakes because, in its eyes, it never makes mistakes. Obviously it has never heard of the requirement to accept the umpire's decision, especially when it's from your own self-appointed umpire. It will continue to behave this way as long as there are no penalties for doing so. Once again, no formal apology was forthcoming from the Managing Director.

Following extensive public criticisms and powerful defences of Wran by a roll-call of former colleagues, including a statement from former ABC Chairman and Managing Director, David Hill, that "the Board must act on editorial failures", Meldrum-Hanna launched into a social media tirade, staunchly defending her actions.

She even tweeted a 'like' of a social media post which was highly critical of senior ABC management, despite the Managing Director having recently warned staff about their behaviour on social media. Once again the ABC and the journalist refused to apologise or make any public comment.

 At least when Sally Neighbour 'liked' a number of Twitter posts mocking Christian Porter, the ABC said the matter was being investigated. But it also added that the outcome would remain confidential, meaning she will never be publicly held to account, and probably not privately either. Neither of these responses is good enough.

The ABC is a publicly owned body. When its "star" reporters go rogue the public is entitled to know how seriously the matters are being treated and what the outcome is, in order to act as a deterrent to others.

Four Corners is a serial offender. A short while back it set out to denigrate the Prime Minister, Scott Morrison, by implying that he was close to an extreme right wing conspiracy-driven group, QAnon, and was doing the bidding of a local sympathiser.

When this exercise backfired badly, the story barely making the news reports the following day, no apology was forthcoming from senior management, leaving the principal offenders, reporter

Louise Milligan and her executive producer Sally Neighbour, free to ignore their own failings.

One of the low lights of Milligan's career has been her obsessive pursuit of Cardinal George Pell. Even in the face of the unanimous acquittal by the High Court, a verdict endorsed by all leading legal authorities, Milligan simply treated the verdict as wrong and continued her vendetta.

The ABC raised no objection to Milligan writing another book, after Pell had been acquitted, in which she continued to imply that Pell remained guilty of a range of offences and suggested that he should not have been able to appeal to the High Court. Although she attempted to cast doubt on the outcome, she was never able to suggest how Pell could have committed the offences.

The ABC's response to the ultimate Pell verdict was churlish but predictable, after having salivated for years at the prospect of him getting what they deemed to be his just deserts. It was very reluctant to mention that the High Court acquittal verdict had been unanimous and was quite happy to allow several of its leading activist/journalists to make the outrageous claim that the result did not mean that Pell was innocent. Not a word of criticism of the deplorable failings of the Victorian legal system, or Daniel Andrews' ill-concealed disgust at the acquittal, let alone the ABC's own rampant shortcomings.

In the early stages of the Trump presidency *Four Corners* spent an inordinate amount of time and money trying to establish that the Trump camp had been in league with Russian operatives ahead of the 2016 presidential election. This all came to nothing when Trump was exonerated by the Special Prosecutor, Robert Mueller, but it made no difference to *Four Corners*, which just ignored the result.

The most recent *Four Corners* debacle was a program masterminded by Sarah Ferguson, recently rewarded with the plum job of hosting *7.30*. Little more than an undergraduate conspiracy theory, it was an attempt to establish that Rupert Murdoch, via News Corp and Fox News, was largely responsible for Donald Trump's 2016 presidential victory, despite abundant evidence of Fox criticisms of Trump's candidacy.

Ferguson simply refused to acknowledge the simple truth – that Hillary Clinton was a dud candidate, contemptuous of millions of middle Americans, while Donald Trump masterfully accommodated their concerns.

Meanwhile, in August 2021, ahead of a special 60th anniversary episode, a fiercely unrepentant Sally Neighbour couldn't help penning a puerile puff piece boasting that *Four Corners* was effectively better than ever, while Ferguson's contribution was similarly awash with self-aggrandisement.

In 2019 the Australian Communications and Media Authority twice criticised the ABC for breaches of its impartiality obligations, but it made no difference – no apology, no retreat – simply business as usual. By now it should be crystal clear that the ABC is out of control, taking no notice of any criticisms, even from the highest quarters.

How does this all this come about? Is it simply the product of a few powerful and effectively untouchable activist journalists free to pursue their personal agendas, or is there a committee process for guidance and sign-off? Is the so-called Editor-in-Chief involved? These matters can be pursued in Senate Estimates but it would be much more satisfactory if the ABC came clean voluntarily.

Given its once-hallowed history *Four Corners* has fallen far. It continues to pride itself on being Australia's leading investigative journalism program but it is hard to recall the last time it uncovered anything worthwhile – it now prefers dirt digging to fact-finding.

In the light of the ABC's continuing intransigence and refusal to accept responsibility for its editorial failures, extreme caution should be exercised before giving undue weight to a belated apology on 7 September 2021 to former senator Cory Bernardi for not giving him a fair opportunity to respond to potentially defamatory allegations prior to broadcast, as required by ABC editorial standard 5.3. By the way, why is John Dawkins not entitled to the same acknowledgement?

There is also no mention of any internal reprimands for senior journalists who were presumably fully aware of their obligations. This apology should therefore be seen as "strategic" – designed to encourage the major parties in the lead up to the election to believe that change was underway and therefore no serious reform proposals were necessary.

RE-LOCATION PROPOSALS

In June 2021, after many years of being encouraged to get its leading political journalists out of their comfortable inner-city cocoon, the ABC suddenly announced an intention to relocate some 300 staff a short half-hour drive from Ultimo to Paramatta by the beginning of 2025 – some three and a half years hence. The timing and lack of substantive detail is very revealing.

It would be well aware that the BBC went down this path years ago with no ill-effects, and Manchester is much further away from city centre than Ultimo. Instead, aware that a Federal election was around the corner and that the patience of its responsible minister, Paul Fletcher, was wearing thin, it decided to appease him by seeming to address one of his prime concerns.

The ABC had already opened a bureau in Parramatta in March 2020 so there is no good reason why some of its key personnel couldn't be relocated there sooner rather than later. It could also have expanded or acquired a nearby facility.

The key reason the Government advocated this change was so that leading political players such as Fran Kelly, Laura Tingle and Leigh Sales could physically relocate themselves and thereby imbibe a new environment and some new ideas closer to the heart of middle Australia.

But the announcement makes no mention of residential relocation, so it is perfectly possible it will be business as usual, with staff simply driving the short distance to Parramatta each day from their inner-city digs. And there is no guarantee that any of its leading lights will "relocate"; the announcement carefully avoided naming names or titles, merely saying that 75% of its "content makers" will be involved.

From her reported comments, Ita Buttrose seemed to think it was all about providing more news about western Sydney, when the object of the exercise was much more about re-shaping the mindset by being exposed to different cultural values and breathing outer suburban air.

As Paul Fletcher had stressed: "More diversity of people will mean more diversity of opinion". But there is no reason to think the ABC is on board with this aim. Time and again it advocates all other forms of diversity, while pretending that it doesn't have a political diversity problem.

PROGRAM QUALITY

Early in my term as Minister for Communications I floated an idea to Quentin Dempster, the ABC's most fervent warrior/defender and enemy of all things conservative. I thought he would like my suggestion that the ABC should aspire to be "the quality alternative to the commercials". Instead, he recoiled in horror.

Perhaps he was afraid the ABC might have to vacate such genres as games shows, cheap and easy program fillers undergraduate quizzes, or "comedy", much of which is low brow, adolescent or simply unfunny. Both of these genres are obvious commercial territory so there is no cultural gap to be filled.

The commercials have to cater for their audiences and feed them accordingly. The Parliament and the people expect the ABC to offer something new and different and generally of a superior quality.

BIAS CONCERNS

Nobel Prize winner, Daniel Kahneman, powerfully demonstrated in his best-selling book, *Thinking, Fast and Slow*, that we all have our biases, although those of journalists are by definition on public display, so they have much greater consequences. Journalists are entitled to have strong political views but they are not entitled to impose them on their audience, especially without giving them enough information to make up their own minds.

People are inquisitive beings. They want to know and understand the world around them. They crave information and explanation. They don't want to be force fed on a politically inspired diet, reflecting the biases and prejudices of the presenter.

Troy Bramston pointedly wrote in the wake of the Luna Park/ Wran disgrace, that despite being found guilty by an impeccable independent enquiry "the ABC has done nothing to correct the record, apologise to Wran's family or respond to an avalanche of criticism by respected individuals".

He could have gone further, as the head of ABC Communications, Sally Jackson, sent him a defiant and unbelievably offensive email saying that she did not feel it necessary to respond to "mere assertions of belief" by a bevy of leading citizens, despite the fact that they had all known Wran well, worked closely with him, and knew his confreres.

Even before the damning report was handed down NSW police

voiced their frustration with the broadcaster's refusal to hand over critical information or to cooperate with an ongoing enquiry into the Luna Park fatality. When the ABC finally agreed to co-operate, it refused to release the report until it had issued a pre-emptive and inaccurate public statement in an unsubtle attempt to blunt the report's impact.

Caro Hanna-Meldrum, the principal reporter for this train wreck of a program, has been defiantly unrepentant, and is clearly in no mood to learn from her mistakes. In any private sector firm she would be long gone by now. Her behaviour makes it painfully clear that she does not regard herself as answerable to any higher authority – a further demonstration of the fact that the ABC has an Editor-in-Chief in name only.

ABC biases are not always party political, although it seems to reserve special venom for any person or organisation it regards as conservative. It is much more a problem of a distinctly left of centre world view, infected with groupthink and a mindset which regards the ABC as a natural monopoly, there as of right, a national treasure to be respected and appreciated but with a God-given right to run its own affairs without any sense of accountability to anyone.

It is an interesting phenomenon to notice how many new arrivals are quickly captured by the group ethos. For example, David Speers and Annabel Crabb both struck me in their pre-ABC days as simply very competent and professional journalists. But once they boarded the ABC cruise ship they seemed to develop a distinctive list to the left.

Crabb now feels the need to write inane opinion pieces such as a response to the 2020 Federal budget headed "Can a Budget shaped by male leaders hope to deliver for the women hit hardest by this recession?"

Speers quickly acquired the ABC obsession, perfected by Leigh Sales, of constant interruption to head off any answer which doesn't fit the ABC agenda. Since joining the ABC Speers has turned this into an unsavoury art form. Not long ago he managed to interrupt Prime Minister Scott Morrison no fewer than 30 times during a 22 minute interview. A few weeks later he interrupted a senior minister, Stuart Robert, on 15 occasions during a 13 minute interview, on the pretext of correcting a non-existent mistake of his own making. He shows no sign of correcting this unprofessional tendency.

Meanwhile, on another program, Ellen Fanning kept interrupting Alexander Downer until he insisted on his right to complete his answer. Leigh Sales is another incorrigible on this front, her favourite line being: "Sorry, if I could just jump in there". When Josh Frydenberg had the temerity to call her out she admitted she wasn't sorry at all.

All these smart alecks are clearly unaware of the measured, non hostile approach adopted by legendary BBC figures such as Robin Aitken, Robin Day, David Dimbleby, David Frost, and Andrew Neil, all of whom were able to elicit useful information while providing memorably high quality interviews. The key question here is why the ABC Editor-in-Chief or the Board won't step in to forestall this demeaning practice of constant interruptions.

Ever dismissive of mainstream public opinion, the ABC presumably thought it was being clever when it chose in January 2021 to use the term Invasion Day interchangeably with Australia Day. It is to be hoped that the furious public response means that this low point will not be repeated – what is certain, however, is that the ABC will never apologise for yet another manifest error of judgment.

Media Watch, hosted by Paul Barry, is an interesting in-house animal. It is certainly not understaffed, with no less than 10 producers and researchers, for a weekly 15 minute program claiming to be holding the media, including the ABC, to account.

Barry deserves considerable commendation for his courage in holding certain high profile ABC journalists to account in the face of a deafening silence from his employers. Perhaps the high watermark of ABC intransigence occurred in 2018 when ACMA adjudged the ABC's leading political presenter, Andrew Probyn, to have breached the organisation's own impartiality standards by calling former prime minister, Tony Abbott, "the most destructive politician of his generation".

ACMA said that this assessment was judgmental and would be understood by the ordinary viewer to be pejorative. ACMA's finding upheld a complaint from an anonymous viewer who had, as required, first complained to the ABC, which came back with the usual 'nothing to see here' response.

The ACMA judgment was devastating:

> "The ABC has a statutory duty to ensure that the gathering and presentation of news and information is impartial according to the recognised standards of objective journalism. Aiming to equip audiences to make up their own minds is consistent with the public sector character of the ABC... Achieving impartiality requires a broadcaster to present material in a way which avoids conveying a prejudgment or giving effect to the affections or enmities of the reporter or presenter".

The ABC obfuscated from start to finish, first pretending that all was OK because it was a climate change story, which was highly newsworthy and in the public interest. But as ACMA pointed out: "The ordinary reasonable viewer would have understood the statement to be a comment on Mr Abbott's political career, rather than a comment specific to his involvement with climate change policy".

ACMA did not have the power to order an apology, which should not have been necessary if the ABC had been prepared to accept the umpire's verdict. A few years earlier, when Jonathan Holmes was in the *Media Watch* chair and was chastised by ACMA, he had the good grace to apologise, saying "In this case we and the ABC accept the umpire's ruling".

In the Probyn case, the ABC supported him every inch of the way, contesting every word, and refusing to apologise or even report the ACMA finding – how contemptuous can you get? To his credit, this was too much even for Paul Barry, who said all this was "a step too far".

Perhaps the reason for the ABC flatly refusing to apologise was that, to its activist journalists, climate change is an article of faith and Tony Abbott was the ultimate *bete noir*, so a craven management simply couldn't afford to antagonise them.

THE BBC LEADS THE WAY

In a significant new development, which could and should be emulated by the ABC, in late October 2021 the BBC announced a comprehensive overhaul of its editorial processes, focussing, inter alia, on the vexed issues of impartiality and whistleblowing.

The BBC's tribulations have been well documented in the wake of the disgraceful Martin Bashir deceit regarding his interview with Diana, Princess of Wales and the subsequent 25 year cover-up, the BBC's backing the wrong horse over Brexit, and the fallout from the Jimmy Savile affair.

In May 2021, the Director-General, Tim Davie, set up a high level review of editorial processes, governance and culture, headed by Sir Nicholas Serota, an impeccable establishment figure, whose report forms the basis for the new approach to a key issue.

The BBC plan recommends clarifications as to how to BBC handles editorial complaints as well as the monitoring of "impartiality metrics".

The BBC is at pains to stress that its "editorial values of impartiality, accuracy and trust are the foundation of our relationship with our audiences". These are the very issues which have caused the ABC, and its audiences, so much heartburn in recent years, largely due to the lack of accountability by its senior journalistic "talent" and the wilful refusal of management to take any positive and meaningful corrective action. As the BBC says "Impartiality is at the heart of the

BBC's mission and public purposes". Accordingly it now proposes to appoint external experts to ensure its content is impartial.

Why can't the same regime apply to the ABC? As Sir Nicholas Serota has said: "the BBC needs to do more to embed editorial values into the fabric of the organisation". So does the ABC.

Such an approach is common sense, simply reflecting the BBC's supposed core values. Yet a similar self-examination inside our/ their ABC would likely be viewed as revolutionary – all the more reason why it is vitally necessary if the ABC is to get back on an even keel and restore its public trust.

What all this amounts to is that the ABC has become a law unto itself, dismissive of government, and contemptuous of any statutory restrictions. It disdains accountability to the Parliament, the regulators or the general public, yet expects ever more public money to come its way, to be spent on whatever whim takes its fancy.

The time has surely come for the Government and the Parliament to ignore the predicable shrieks of "independence" and only provide funding for clearly spelt out projects, subject to continuing parliamentary oversight. The ABC should be required to submit a Request for Funding document which should spell out its needs/ wants and be made public.

THE COMPLAINTS REGIME

Only recently we had yet another typical example of how senior staff have no idea of what "proper standards of governance" really means.

In August 2021 a former Liberal staffer complained to the ABC about Louise Milligan's unauthorised exposure of her as a source and misrepresentation of her in a tweet. But instead of providing a substantive reply, the ABC complaints department washed its hands of the matter on the grounds that it was a personal tweet and referred it to Milligan's boss, Sally Neighbour. She wrote back to say that she had looked into the matter and spoken to Milligan and "I am satisfied that there has been no misconduct by Ms Milligan" – a classic case of the offender being judge and jury in its own cause.

No analysis was offered or reasons given. The blatant conflict of interest was ignored. Neighbour was either ignorant of the concept or just hoped no one would notice. Not before time, in March 2022 the ABC quietly let it be known that Neighbour was leaving the organisation. No word, of course, about any generous golden handshake to ensure she doesn't spill any beans once free from the mothership.

The most fundamental problem with the current rules is that the ABC has a massive conflict of interest. Instead of a complaint being judged by an independent authority, as other public sector organisations such as the police have been required to do for many years, a public complaint must first be directed to the ABC's in-house Audience and Consumer Affairs unit, whose role is "to review and, where appropriate, investigate complaints alleging that ABC content has breached the ABC's editorial standards".

It does not have to make a determination – it may simply deal with it "in some other more appropriate way...If we don't accept your complaint for investigation, we will often refer it to the relevant area of the ABC and ask them to respond to you directly" – no reasons given. Again, Caesar judging Caesar.

There are no guarantees about timely replies: "Audience and Consumer Affairs aim to respond within 30 days of receiving your complaint, but some matters will take longer to finalise".

There are further get-out clauses: "Where Audience and Consumer Affairs accepts a complaint for investigation, it will consider the seriousness and complexity of the matter to determine the resources and nature of response that may be required. The extent of resources applied to complaint investigations will be proportionate to the nature of the complaint".

In other words, the ABC is able to take as long as it likes and do as it likes, and time is on its side, as many complainants will get sick of waiting and give up. Even worse, the ABC can simply claim that the complaint is inappropriate or too complex – end of story. None of this would happen if a speedy, external and impartial adjudication process was in place.

Finally, in the face of an avalanche of criticism, the ABC resorted to what smelled like a brazen pre-emptive proposal to head off any meaningful change. On 17 October 2021 the Chairman, Ita Buttrose, announced that the Board had commissioned an "independent" review of its in-house complaints process to be completed by March 2022.

The strategy was crystal clear: come up with some modest changes ahead of an imminent Federal election, keep firm in-house control of the process and claim the problem had been solved before the next Government could put in place a genuinely arm's-length decision-making regime, not involving the ABC, save for having the opportunity to put its side of the case.

However, no doubt to the ABC's surprise and disappointment, the independent review was nobody's lapdog. On 17 May 2022 it delivered its report, which found that the existing complaints process was in need of major changes: "Our impression is that there are public misgivings about key aspects of the complaints process that are soundly based, and as such there is considerable scope for improvement". It made 11 recommendations, which have already been adopted by the board. As one commentator sagely observed the current system effectively allowed the ABC to "mark its own homework".

The reviewers are to be commended for their political courage in stating the bleeding obvious, which has been blindingly apparent to outsiders for nearly thirty years. Ita Buttrose is also to be commended for at last, perhaps unwittingly, lancing the boil.

However, this where the trouble begins. A key recommendation is for the appointment of an ABC ombudsman to lead the existing complaints-handling unit and reporting direct to the board. It is not known who is to make the appointment because the ABC has not yet allowed the review to be publicly released but there is little no doubt it will be the ABC. Indeed, the Review states explicitly that "The ombudsman will report direct to the board".

This is simply not good enough, as there is still no arm's length separation. Such person will be very quickly captured by the ABC ethos and therefore the proposal does not satisfy the by now standard requirement for transparency.

The review also made other stinging findings:

- The way the ABC handles complaints from the public about inappropriate social media commentary by staff should be revised.... Personal social media accounts should not be used in a way that facilitates even a perception of ABC bias.
- The ABC was not as forthcoming as it should be when admitting to editorial mistakes...and in issuing an apology in response to an adverse ruling.

Both of these findings are masterpieces of understatement as the Reviewers would well have known that the ABC's repeated conduct was flagrant and contumelious – in other words, scornful and insulting, even insolent.

THE APPOINTMENT OF AN ABC OMBUDSMAN

It is therefore high time that the ABC itself was held to account by a government-appointed, arms-length, independent Ombudsman, to whom complainants can have speedy and direct access.

The ombudsman would be an independent adjudicator. The ABC's only role in the process would be to promptly provide any facts or information requested by the Ombudsman and to make submissions justifying and explaining the reasons for its actions – in other words, a right to be heard.

Subject to any particular sensitivities, the Ombudsman should publish its decision, outlining the nature of the complaint, its findings, the reasons for same and any appropriate sanctions. There should also be a right of appeal to ACMA on a point of law, with a power to refer the matter back to the Ombudsman for reconsideration.

Ita Buttrose has not scornfully rejected the idea, as most of her in-house minions would no doubt have done. Instead, she said it was "an interesting idea" and "we'd be interested to see whether Australians share that point of view" – commendably open-minded.

As an independent media oversight body, the Ombudsman should have the right to require the ABC to provide a meaningful, non-querulous response to complaints and, where appropriate, a public explanation, justification or apology.

Most importantly, it should have the power to impose fines, if necessary heavy ones. Given its contemptuous dismissal of even ACMA findings, this is the only language the ABC understands.

The ABC itself should long ago have been acutely aware of the critical importance of arm's-length, wholly independent decision-making processes but, as it has continued to resolutely resist any attempts to be held accountable and treats criticisms and even formal findings with disdain, it has run out of time to reform itself.

An Ombudsman is typically appointed by a parliamentary body to represent the public regarding to the conduct of governmental agencies; they conduct formal investigations. A News Ombudsman is an independent officer acting in the best interests of news consumers and as a mediator between the expectations of the public and the responsibilities of journalists.

A government-appointed Ombudsman is probably the single most important measure a Federal Government could take to rein in the ABC and get it back on track. According to research commissioned by the Menzies Research Centre, it would have the support of four out of five Australians, with more than 80% of Labor and Greens voters in favour.

THE IRAQ WAR FIASCO

The ABC's self-serving, self-judging ploy is not a new phenomenon, as I know from my time as minister. It is now nearly two decades since my monumental run-in over AM's anti-American coverage of the Iraq war in 2003. Much has changed in the world since then, but one thing that has not changed in the slightest is the overweening cultural and political conceit of the national broadcaster.

Of my 68 complaints two were upheld by the ABC's in-house complaints manager, who sneeringly dismissed the remainder with gratuitous and totally unbecoming language. He was not the only ABC employee to weigh in. David Marr, then the presenter of the ABC TV *Media Watch*, almost immediately resorted to ridicule.

When I criticised this self-serving outcome the ABC, without reference to me, referred the matter to an ABC-appointed Independent Complaints Review Panel, which, lo and behold, upheld another 15 – a massive ABC own goal.

The ABC in-house response was extreme. David Marr, together with Linda Mottram who had presented most of the offending items, were both heavily critical of the ABC-appointed Panel and questioned its integrity, happy to defy the Managing Director's public proclamation that "any questioning of the integrity and credibility of ICRP members was nothing short of offensive". Once again, it was clear that management lacked authority.

In due course I asked the Australian Broadcasting Authority to further consider the matter and it duly found another four instances in which the ABC had breached its own Code of Practice. Once again, the ABC's in-house warriors did their worst, with David Marr using almost his entire *Media Watch* program to unload an avalanche of invective, accusing the ABA of being both "slovenly" and "dishonest".

To its credit the ABA was undeterred, firmly but politely saying that "when a program uses tendentious language in connection with a controversial matter, listeners are entitled to understand that the program favours a particular view of the issue". It went on to say that: "The ABA considers that the findings of 17 breaches of editorial standards...plus the four code breaches found by the ABA compromised the quality of *AM*'s coverage of the Iraq War".

Unbelievably, this devastating indictment of the ABC's professionalism was met with a deafening silence from the Chairman and the Managing Director, but not from Mottram, who again unleashed an angry and defiant response. Finally, almost two years after the events in question, the Managing Director, Russell Balding, had the temerity to publicly claim that the ABC had been vindicated by the ABA! He offered no apology or any rational explanation – just mountains of undergraduate level spin.

In all, a total of 21 complaints had been upheld – one a day for the 21 days of the Iraq War! Yet the ABC never acknowledged these calamitous findings – deathly silence, no apology or explanation, happy to let sympathetic journalists claim that I had effectively lost because a majority of my complaints had not been upheld!

What strikes me as most significant is that once David Marr resigned from the ABC his belligerent attitude changed completely. No longer the staunch warrior/defender of the tribe, he wrote in the *Sydney Morning Herald*: "the only clear win for the ABC would be exoneration of (sic) just about every count. That's not what happened. The former minister for communications, Richard Alston, has seen more than a third of his complaints upheld".

When put together with the furious and aggressive responses from others, right up to the Managing Director, it is clear that a herd, and even coercive, mentality prevailed then and, as recent events have amply demonstrated, it is still alive and well today.

This is not merely group think, where everyone is of like mind. It has the appearances of something more sinister – a belief that almost any outrage will quickly blow over, plus a fear of upsetting the troops, who will be only too quick to defenestrate any one inclined to stray from the defence orthodoxy. United We Stand...

What becomes blindingly clear in all this is that the ABC has become a law unto itself. Despite being officially required to act as a "model litigant", its behaviour is the very opposite – not only does it refuse to accept any independent umpire's verdict but simply digs in and attempts to muddy the waters. Its whole modus operandi is to make the problem go away without ever properly and honestly analysing the issue or seeking to remedy the deficiency.

A MAJOR SOURCE OF THE PROBLEM

There are clearly deep-seated problems with the ABC and its complaints handling procedures which go back a long way. But we could do a lot worse in seeking to understand its attitude of rank superiority, if we look at the career of one its most senior executives who still seeks to influence and, in some senses, distort its compliance obligations.

Long serving ABC senior executive Alan Sunderland was in charge of editorial policies at the ABC from 2013 to 2019, in a range of positions including Head of Editorial Policies, Director of Editorial Policies and Editorial Director. Although he has since officially moved on, he boasts, as recently as July 2021, that "I am still involved from time to time in critiquing the ABC's output". The self-regard is epic and the superiority complex has clearly infected the ABC.

He is a self-proclaimed expert on editorial ethics so his views are critically important to understanding the organisational mindset and why it seems to treat its statutory obligations as mere words without any professional consequences.

If we really want to understand the ABC mindset we can do no better than look at an article he wrote in the *Sydney Morning Herald* in 2017, while still at the ABC, entitled "What's wrong with being fair and balanced?"

He started by acknowledging that the ABC Act does require it to present news and information that is accurate and impartial, according to the recognised standards of objective journalism. But he seemed to think that these last words are a crucial qualifier which negate the ordinary meaning of "accurate and impartial".

He then made the astonishing claim that "when it comes to fair and honest dealing sometimes deception or the breach of an undertaking might be justified in the public interest".

He further asserted that when it comes to "balance", impartiality does not require that every perspective receives equal time, as one of the hallmarks of good journalism is balance that "follows the weight of evidence". What he means by this is that a journalist who puts both sides of the argument is abdicating responsibility to form their own subjective judgment.

He gives an example: "If I write a story that says a doctor wants to vaccinate a child at risk of whooping cough to protect her from harm but the child's mother is refusing because the vaccination will do more harm than good I have produced a piece of writing that is a long way from being responsible journalism", notwithstanding that it is fair to both sides and entirely balanced.

This is Alice in Wonderland stuff. Intelligent readers are entitled to know why the mother is refusing yet Sunderland seems to think that this is not only irrelevant, but irresponsible, and that only the doctor's side of the argument is morally acceptable.

In other words, ABC journalists have no obligation to present both sides of a story or to explain what an issue is all about. Instead they have licence to put their own spin on any and every issue – the very antithesis of what people expect from a national broadcaster.

Yet far from acknowledging any problem with the ABC's response to its multitude of high level complaints, Sunderland continues to stoutly defend the regime, largely on the basis of what he sees as the "efficiency" of the system.

He even goes so far as to say that "it seems unreasonable to deny it is the most efficient, extensive and thorough complaints process anywhere in the Australia media landscape". Not a word about impartiality and integrity, let alone accuracy, fairness and balance – he truly lives in a bureaucrat's supply-side world, impervious to the impact on consumers.

He obviously sees nothing wrong with the ABC judging itself. Accordingly, it is not surprising that this warped thinking still permeates the upper reaches of the organisation. If the ABC is to retrieve its fast declining reputation it should immediately cut all ties to this Svengali figure.

EDITORIAL STANDARDS

A crucial factor which the ABC never acknowledges, but which infects its handling of key issues, is the distinction between a hard and a soft interview, an interesting variant of which is one ABC journalist interviewing another ABC journalist, inevitably of the same view. In many respects this goes to the heart of the problem. The ABC delights in serving up endless stories about the plight of women, indigenous disadvantage, climate change and asylum seekers, always in a wholly sympathetic manner, encouraging the audience to conclude that the Coalition Government is callous and uncaring about imminent disaster. To ABC true believers these are simply self-evident truths, which do not needed to be examined, analysed or debated.

The science of climate change is far from being "settled", as the International Climate Change Committee implicitly acknowledges in regular updates of its findings and projections. There are many logical and sensible alternative views but the ABC simply refuses to mention them, presumably because it has some sort of moral objection, *a la* Sunderland.

Not only that, but it manages to turn every out-of-the-ordinary weather event into a further example of the climate devastation to come. It never explores policy alternatives or adaptation strategies; just pours on the fear. The choice of interviewees is a calculated political decision. That is why Australians never hear the other side of important policy issues.

If we manage to plough through all the ABC policies, rules and standards, they seem to cover all the bases, but when it comes to execution and enforcement, it is a very different matter.

All this is reminiscent of how public bodies can claim black is white and fool a fair proportion of the population. In the old Soviet Union, all leaders claimed they were "perfecting democracy". Stalin, in his notorious 1936 constitution, declared the Soviet Union to be the most democratic country in the world, as did Brezhnev in his 1977 constitution.

East Germany was officially known as the German Democratic Republic. Even today many dictatorships such as North Korea, Algeria, Congo-Kinshasa, Ethiopia, Laos and Nepal use the term "democratic republic".

This goes to the heart of the problem – the ABC feels free to ignore the ordinary meaning of the prescribed rules and to decide that it is free to promote its own subjective views. So if journalists have been brought up on an unrelieved media studies-promoted anti-establishment view and are imbued with comfortable left wing, inner city values, they have no obligation to be objective, but can simply deliver an endless diet of political propaganda.

The ABC is able to get away with this dismissive and self-serving approach for two main reasons:

- a series of complex rules around the complaints regime which effectively allow it to be judge and jury in its own cause.
- a fortress mentality, combined with a lack of effective editorial processes, which enable silos such as *Four Corners, Q& A,* Radio National and Current Affairs to act with impunity and cower senior management into inaction.

INTERNATIONAL EXPERIENCE

There are certain principles accepted by broadcasters in democracies world-wide in assessing compliance with journalistic standards but, as the US does not have a national publicly owned broadcaster, there are only two key jurisdictions which are most relevant to Australia – the UK and Canada. New Zealand has a Chief Ombudsman appointed by the Parliament covering public sector agencies but with no specific national broadcaster responsibility.

In the UK, where, unlike Australia, the national broadcaster remains the UK's primary source for news, the principal regulator is Ofcom, which publishes an annual review of BBC news and current affairs. Its remit is on overall performance and not editorial matters, pointing out that the BBC Board is responsible for overall governance and for ensuring that the BBC delivers its Mission and Public Purposes as set out in the Charter.

While the BBC's claim to media dominance cannot be said of the ABC, there is, however, a content similarity. As Ofcom has pointed out: "Audiences perceived the BBC as giving too much coverage to extreme voices, while others criticised 'false equivalence' in its reporting". In Australia the criticism would extend to obsessions with fashionable themes such as climate change, gender equity, asylum seekers, endemic racism and worker's entitlements, at the expense of any worthwhile coverage of everyday concerns.

Canada has had a dedicated ombudsman for overseeing the

operations and activities of its national broadcaster, CBC/ Radio-Canada, since 1992. However, the position is filled by the Corporation itself and the Ombudsman reports directly to the President and CEO.

Moreover, the Ombudsman only acts as an appeal authority, thereby often significantly delaying the whole process and discouraging all but the most persistent complainant from staying the course. This may have been acceptable 30 years ago but modern best practice demands complete arms-length decision-making, with speedy direct-access and effective oversight arrangements.

Like all national broadcasters, the CBC is required to respect fundamental principles such as impartiality and integrity and most particularly accuracy, fairness and balance in politics, economics and social and cultural issues. In marked contrast, "our" ABC claims that fairness and balance have never been recognised as standards of objective journalism, despite the Canadians having no trouble with the concept!

THE ART OF THE APOLOGY

At least the BBC seems to understand the need for fessing up when caught out, although maybe only when confronted by a very wealthy and respected household name.

I have just finished reading the inspiring autobiography of James Dyson, now Britain's richest man after a lifetime of relentless invention and innovation, which is both insightful and instructive.

His degree of essentially sensible and calculated risk taking is in marked contrast to that of national broadcasters such as the ABC and the BBC and especially their 'star' journalists – they no longer like to be called reporters because it might curtail their freelance activism.

In their desperation to make a name for themselves and come up with big revelations, they constantly engage in what might be called "creative journalism", where the object of the exercise is to convert a mundane story into a scandal – it's called a 'beat up' in the trade, as the ABC would well know.

In April 2021, as Dyson tells it, the BBC "twisted the truth", and as a result the prime minister, Boris Johnson, and himself were "implicated in 'sleaze' ". Dyson stood accused of 'lobbying' the Prime Minister (clearly a hanging offence!) when he was actually only responding to an approach from the latter.

Moreover, even more sinister, he was portrayed as "a

prominent Conservative supporter" on the basis of publicly disclosed modest donations (of less than AUD 20,000) made by his charitable foundation to the Wiltshire Engineering Festival.

Dyson no doubt enjoyed pointing out that he had never attended even a Conservative Party social event and did not give as much as a penny to the Vote Leave campaign, of which he was a prominent supporter.

In the face of these strident denials the BBC had no choice but to issue the following grovelling apology: "We accept that Sir James Dyson is not a prominent Conservative supporter... and made a charitable gift to support the Wiltshire Engineering Festival for school children.

We accept that this does not signal affiliation to any political party and we would like to put the record straight...We wish to make it clear that Sir James contacted Number 10 in response to the Prime Minister's direct request to him. We are sorry that these facts were not always reflected in our coverage and we apologise for not doing so".

Well there you have it – a model, rolled gold and well deserved apology – Sir James could not have drafted it better himself!

THE WAY AHEAD

The ABC should be exposed to competitive funding for special programs such as Australian history, drama and documentaries.

The ABC Charter should be amended to make it clear that the words "fair and balanced" and "accurate and impartial" should have their everyday, common sense meaning and specifically repudiate the noxious Sutherland interpretation.

In line with the findings of the ABC's own commissioned Blackburn report, all current affairs programs should be required to ensure a diversity of voices and political opinion and any complaints of failure to do so should be the direct responsibility of the ACMA, with appropriate enforcement powers.

The ABC's annual expenditure should be subject to independent audit processes, with the results to be tabled in the Parliament.

The position of a staff-appointed director to the ABC Board constitutes a fundamental conflict-of-interest and should be abolished.

The ABC should no longer be able to adjudicate on any complaints against it. This should be the responsibility of an independent, government-appointed Ombudsman with adequate powers of enforcement.

Where a complaint is made, the ABC should be accorded

an opportunity to respond but otherwise play no part in the consideration of the matter.

Where final findings have been made against the ABC it should be obliged to accept them and comply with them and, where requested to do so, apologise and report prominently and in good faith on all its main media outlets.

There should be a right of appeal on a point of law to ACMA from the decisions of the Ombudsman.

The ABC Managing Director should not also hold the position of Editor-in-Chief. It should be the full-time responsibility of an ABC employee. The ABC Charter should define the nature and extent of the ABC's "independence".

The Charter should also be amended to restore the obligation of staff to be accountable to stakeholders and to require senior management to ensure that this occurs.

ABC employees should not be permitted to express personal political opinions in any media outlet or post on any social media platforms and should not be permitted to make public comments critical of the organisation. They should not be indemnified by the ABC for non-work related postings or public statements.

When even long serving employees are leaving the organisation they should not be given any golden handshakes or be subject to any limitations on their right to speak publicly after their departure.

The ABC should be required to adopt a rigorous due diligence and review process before programming contentious matters.

In order to ensure pre-publication accuracy the ABC should be required to adopt industry best practice by double checking and verifying sources and giving subjects of potential criticism a right of reply.

The ABC should be required to set Key Performance Indicators for all senior executive or journalist positions, which should be taken into account in assessing salary levels. No bonuses should be paid.

The ABC should be required to annually report, publicly and in detail, on the extent to which it has become more efficient and responsive to community needs and preferences.

The ABC should be required to table audience performance reports in the Parliament so that taxpayers and the general public can be confident that they are getting value for money.

In line with a recent BBC directive, the ABC should be required to ensure the highest standards of impartiality.

Other than in respect of consumer complaints, allegations of failure to comply with its Charter obligations should be dealt with by ACMA, with the ABC having a right to respond in due course but not to be involved in any adjudication of the matter.   .

ACMA should be empowered, where it has determined that the ABC's actions or conduct amount to a serious invasion of a complainant's privacy, to make an enforceable declaration that the complainant is entitled to a specified amount of compensation.

ACMA's enforcement powers to deal with breaches of the code should be strengthened so that it can require the ABC to take specified remedial action, including a public apology and, where appropriate, impose meaningful financial and other penalties for failure to do so.

Following on from its announcement of relocation proposals, the ABC should be required to expedite the process to encourage a reasonable number of its leading journalists to be physically relocated to the Parramatta area and not simply able to commute from Sydney.

BIBLIOGRAPHY

ABA Report, 1 March 2005.

ABC Public Report on Audience Comments and Complaints, October-December 2003.

ABC statement on Editorial Review: Impartiality of the Federal Election 2019, December 10, 2020.

ACMA Media Release, May 1, 2018.

Troy Bramston, "ABC must apologise for dodgy ghost train doco", *The Australian,* August 30, 2021.

Nick Cater, "The Radicalisation of the ABC, *The Australian,* April 22. 2013.

Henry Ergas, "Public Interest? The ABC Betrays its Founding Principles". *The Australian*, November 12, 2020.

Paul Fletcher to Ita Buttrose, Letter, November 30, 2020. (Letter in full on Paul Fletcher's Twitter Feed).

Four Corners - Trump Russia Parts 1, 2 & 3, Three-part investigative special series reported and presented by Sarah Ferguson, ABC 1, August-September 2021.

Daniel Kahneman, *Thinking, Fast and Slow,* Penguin UK, 2012.

Christopher Lasch, *The Revolt of the Elites and the Betrayal of Democracy,* WW Norton, 1996.

James Madden, "Adding conservative voices 'dangerous'", *The*

Australian, December 12, 2020.

Louise Milligan, *Witness,* Hachette Australia, 2020.

Christian Porter, Resignation Press Release, September 20, 2021

Jonathan Sacks, "Paradoxes of Pluralism", Reith Lectures, December 5, 1990, Radio 4.

The Serota Review, BBC editorial processes, governance, and culture, October 29, 2021.

Benjamin Storey and Jenna Silber Storey, *Why We Are Restless: On the Modern Quest for Contentment* (New Forum Books, 69), Princeton University Press, 2021.

Tom Switzer, "Instinctive Bias Not Among the ABC's Virtues", *The Australian*, January 21, 2007.

Tony Wright, "The ABC is Letting Australia Down", *Sydney Morning Herald,* November 25, 2016.

Lightning Source UK Ltd.
Milton Keynes UK
UKHW042109050922
408358UK00011B/384